THE PROOF

THE PROOF

FIRST AND FRENCH EDITION: © MARVAL 1996, ISBN 2-86234-211-4
ENGLISH EDITION: © DEWI LEWIS PUBLISHING 1996, 8 BROOMFIELD ROAD, HEATON MOOR, STOCKPORT SK4 4ND, 0161 442 9450, ISBN 1 899235 50 7
GERMAN EDITION: © EDITION BRAUS 1997, ISBN 3-89466-177-1

JEAN-PHILIPPE REVERDOT

THE PROOF

DEWI LEWIS

PUBLISHING

facing

the worst

until laughter

burst

Samuel Beckett

1

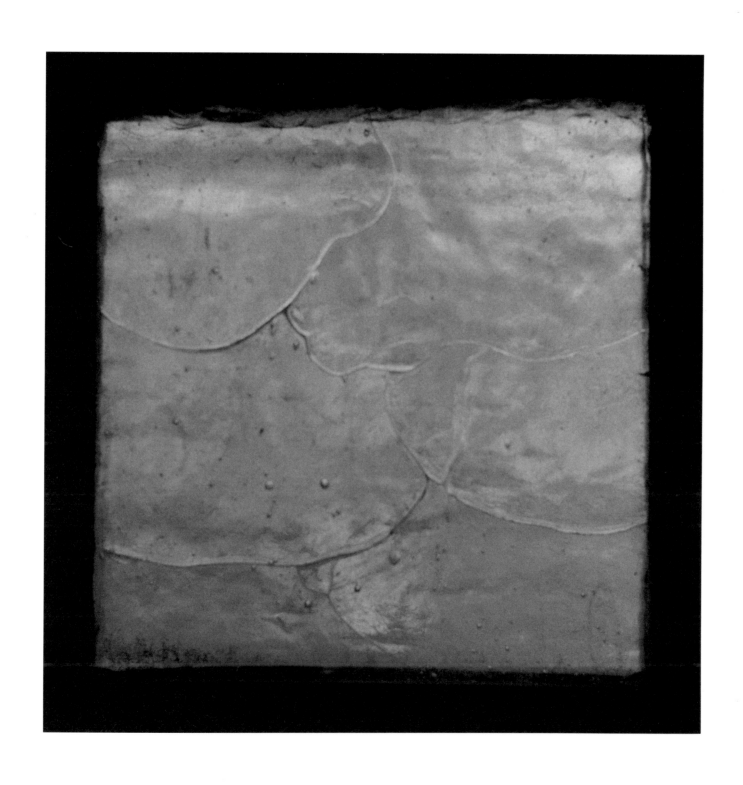

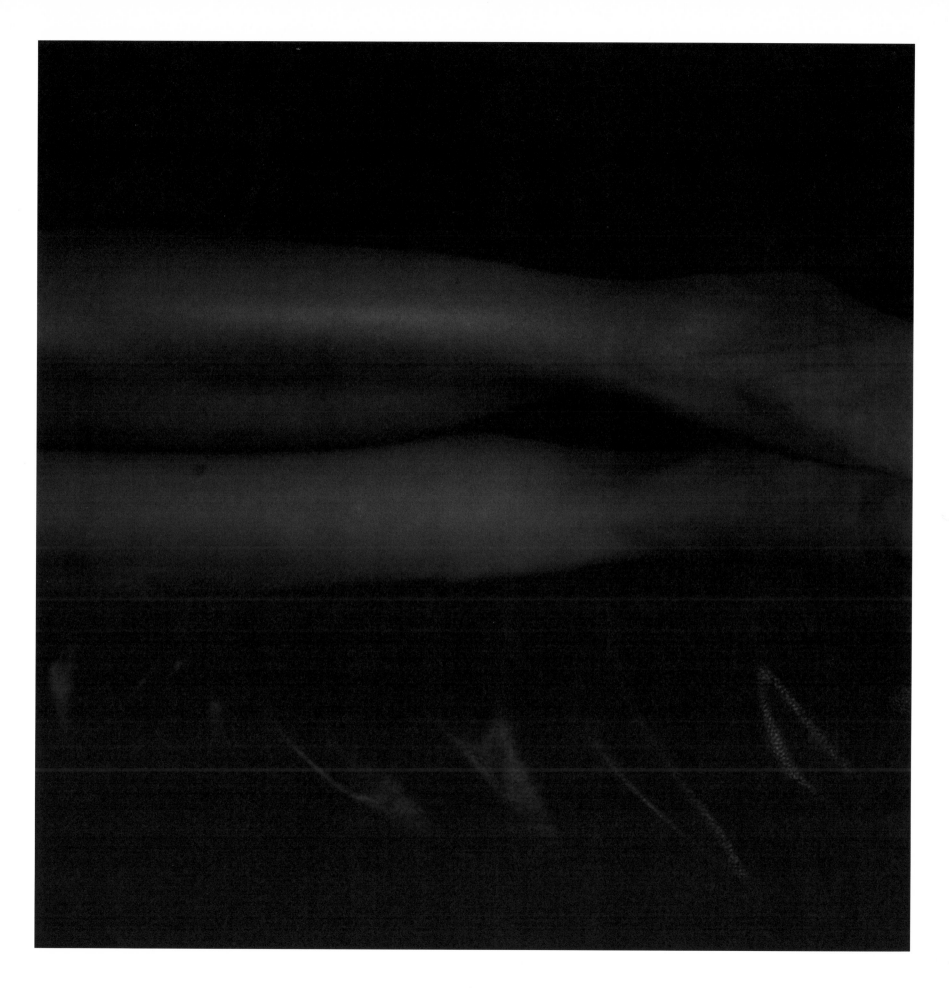

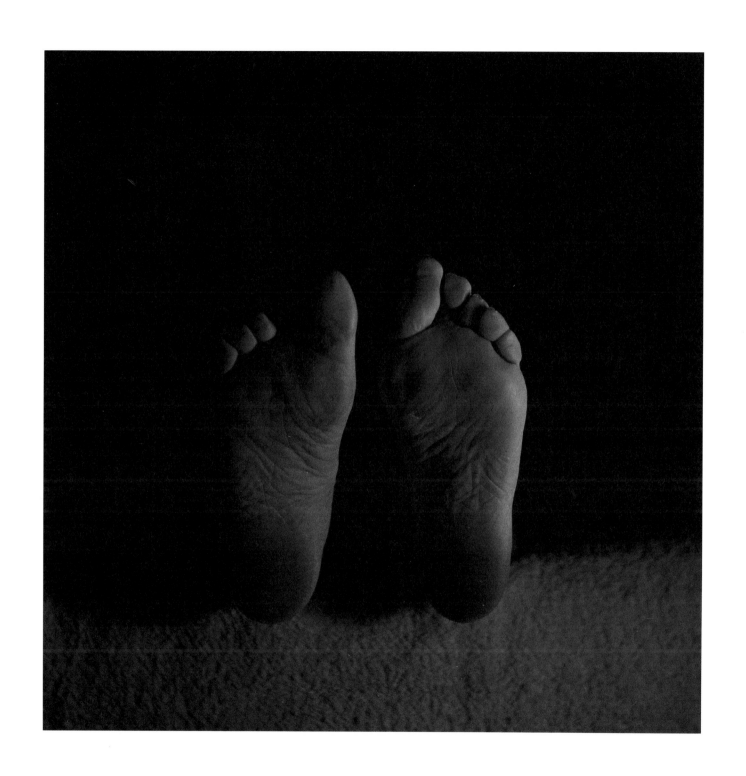

2

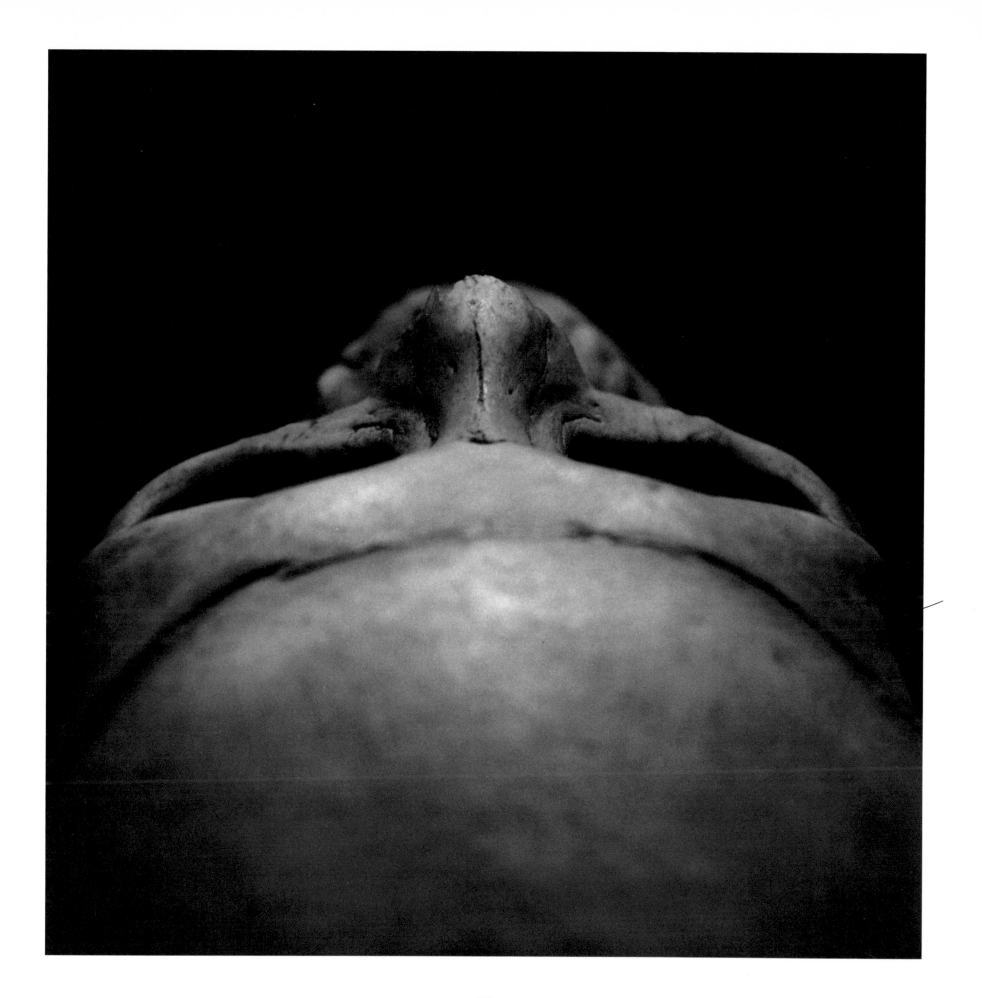

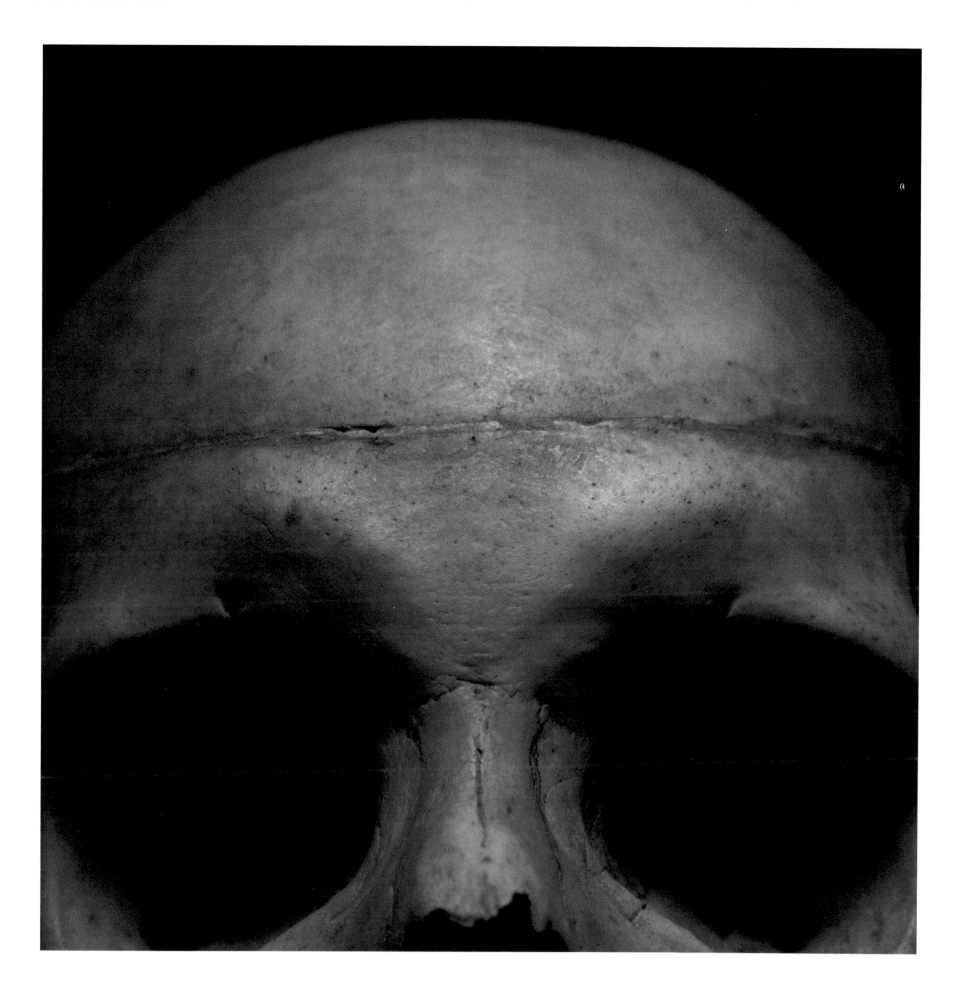

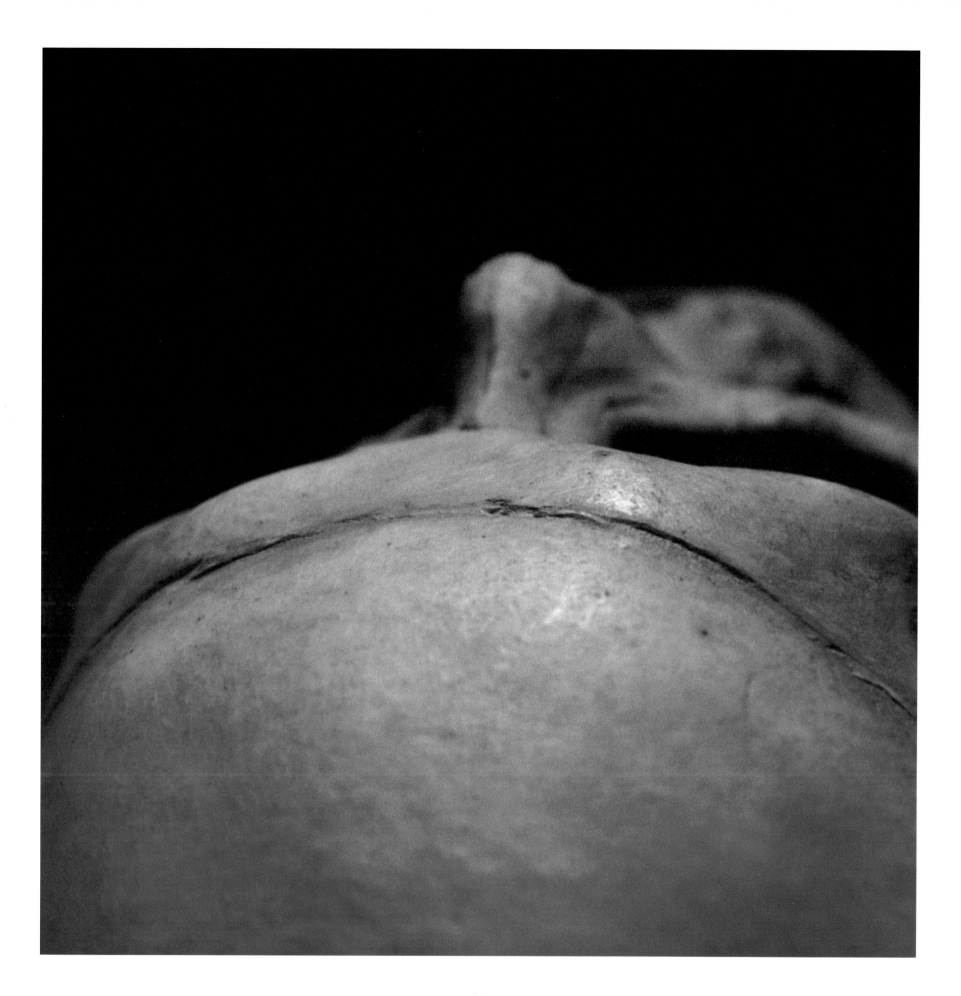

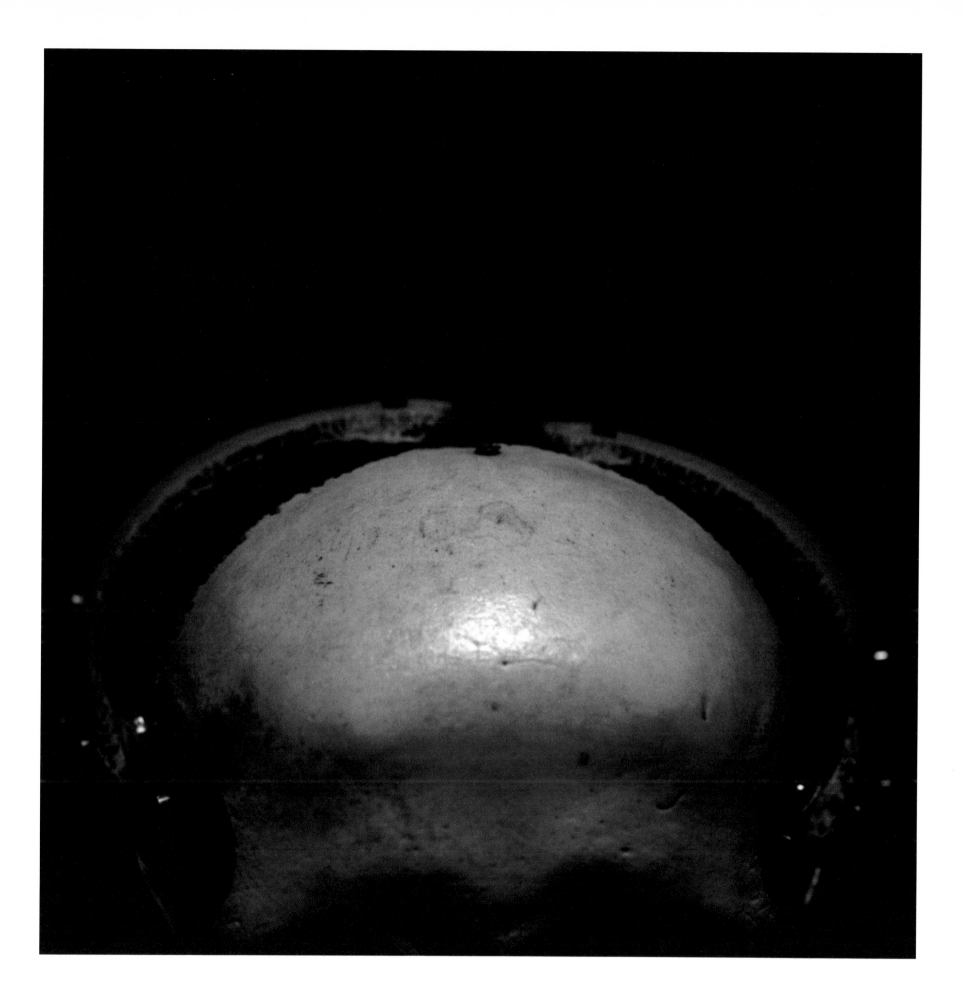

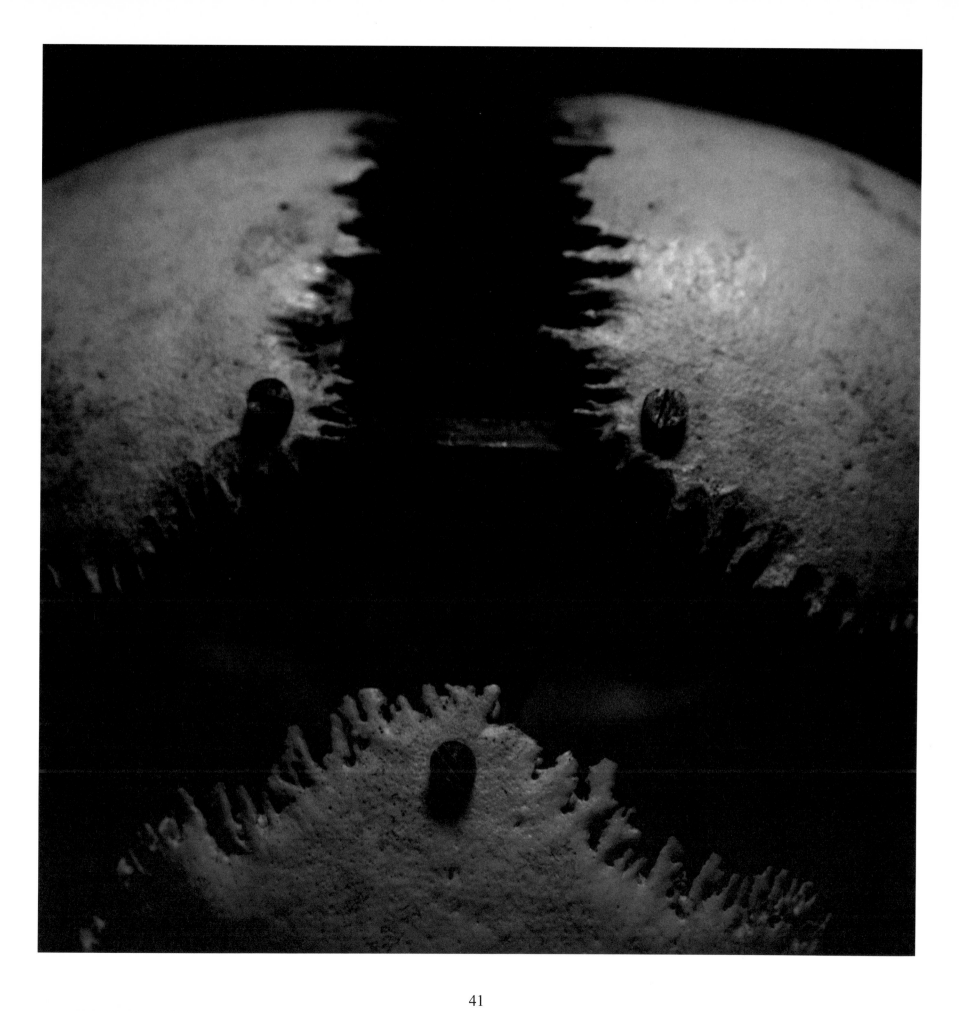

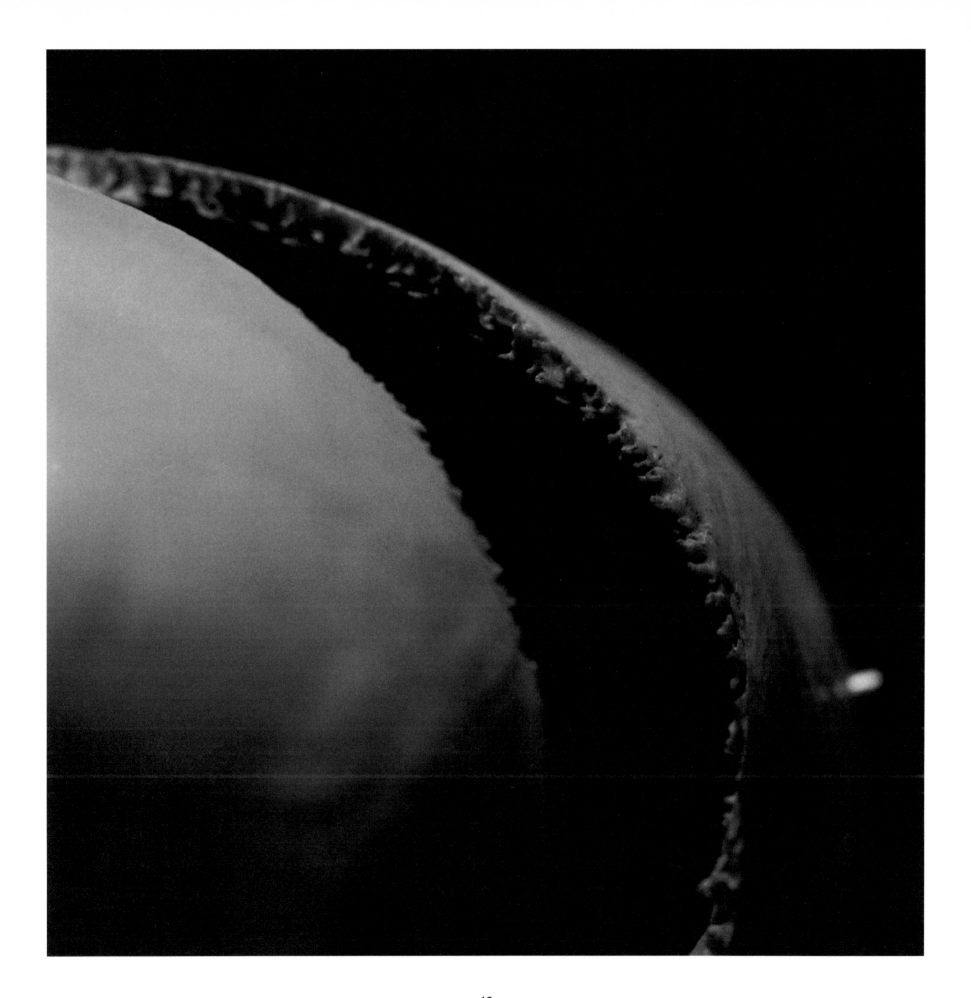

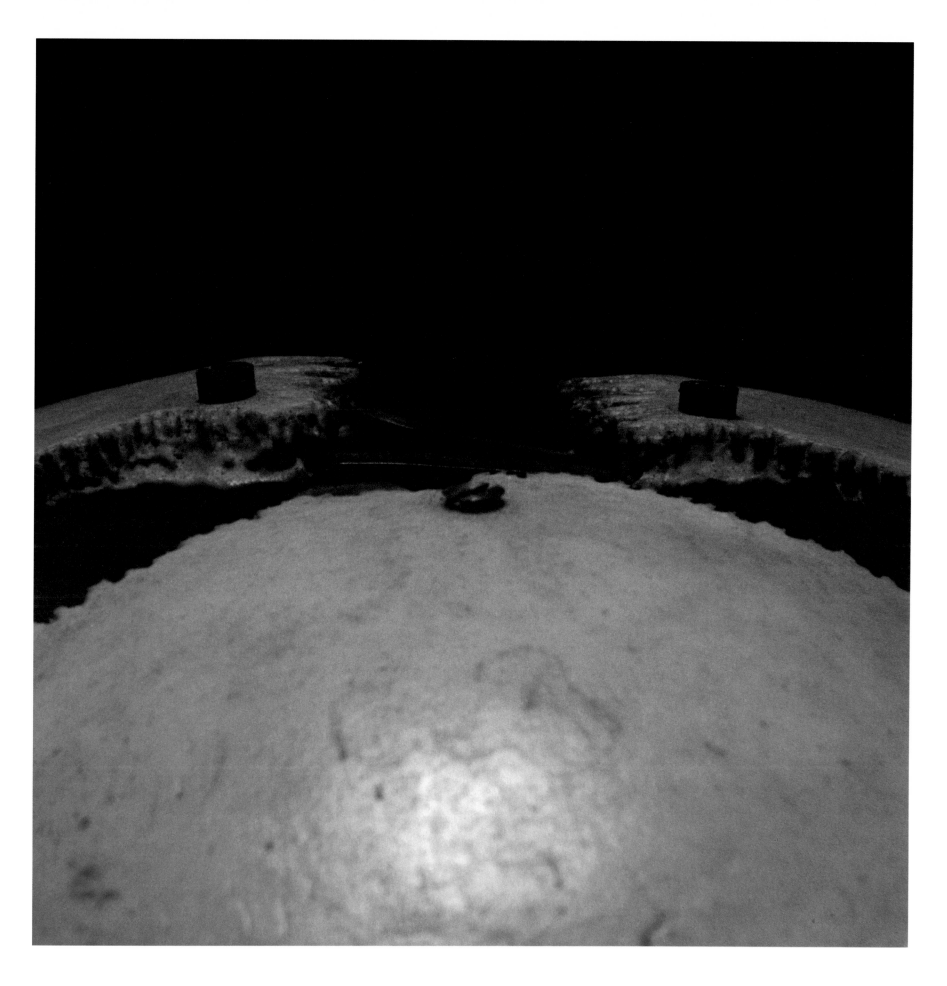

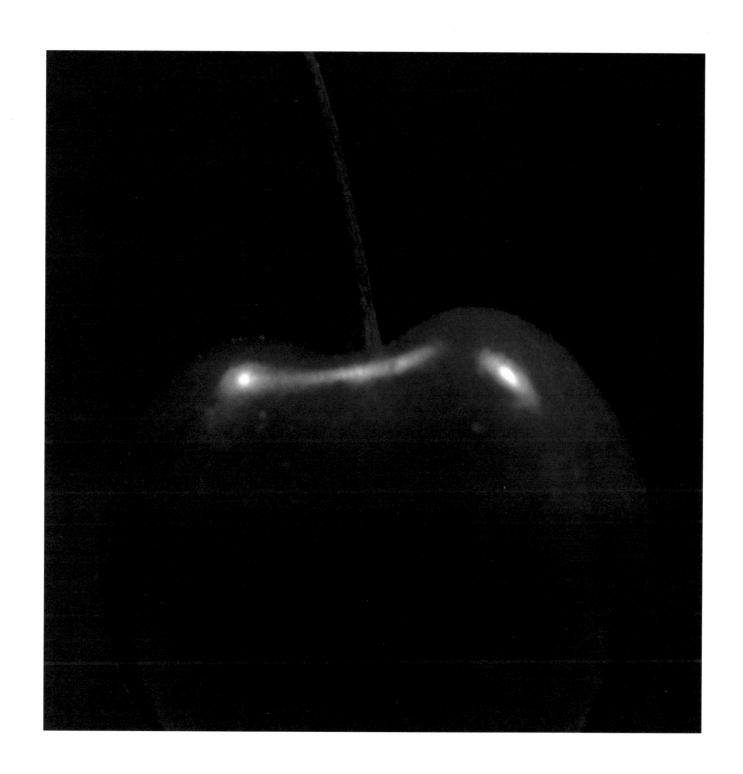

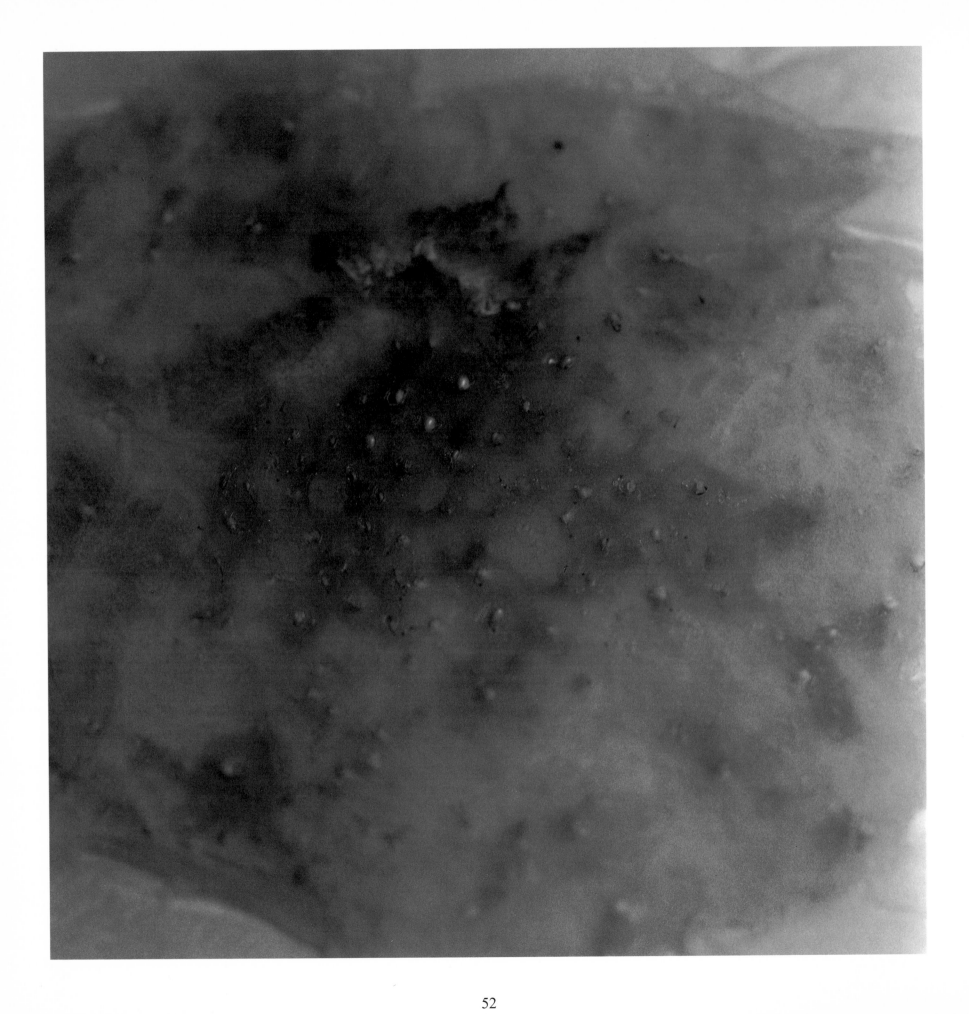

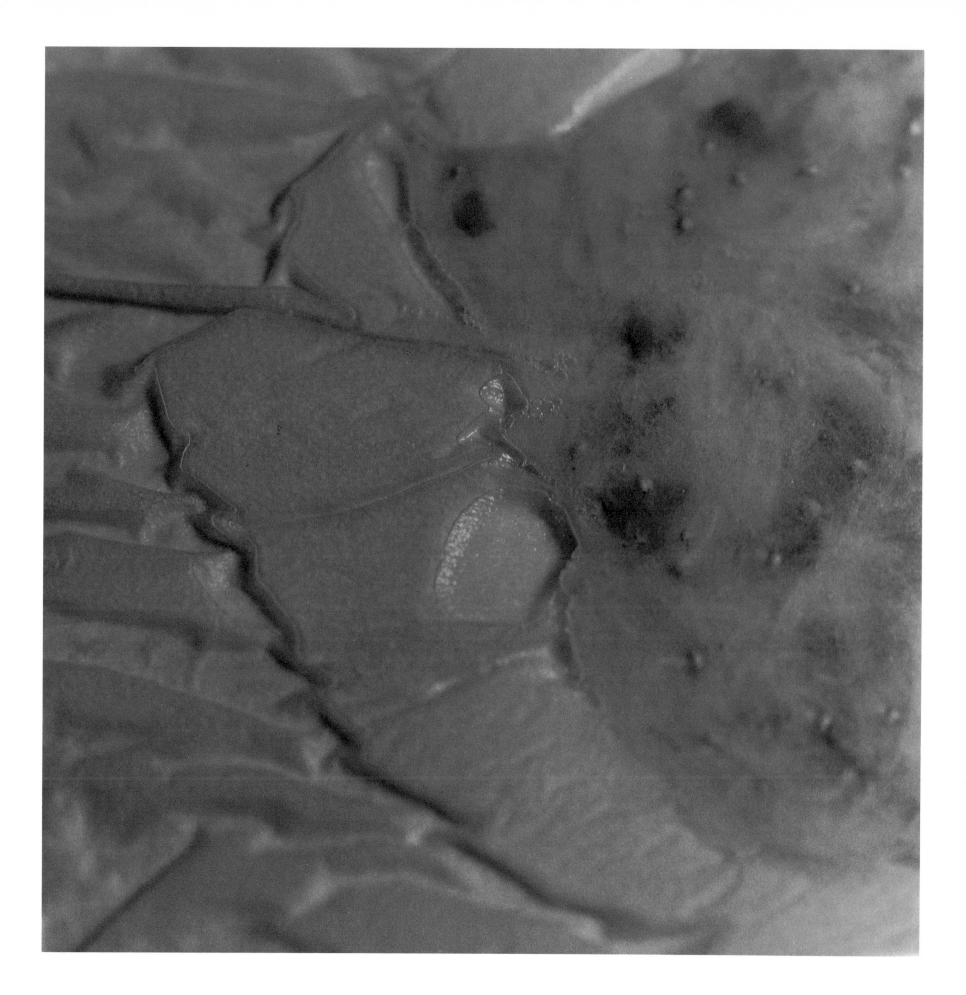